Voyager
Passport C

2

Fluency

ISBN 978-1-4168-0364-5

Printed in the United States of America   08 09 10 11 12 13   CMM   9 8 7 6 5 4 3 2

Table of Contents

Fluency Practice

 Read the story to each other.

 Read the story on your own.

 Read the story to your partner again. Try to read the story even better.

 Questions? Ask your partner two questions about the story. Tell each other about the story you just read.

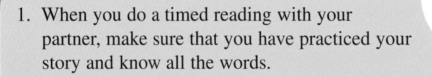
Timed Reading

1. When you do a timed reading with your partner, make sure that you have practiced your story and know all the words.

2. When you are ready, tell your partner to start the timer.

3. Read carefully, and your partner will stop you at 1 minute. When you stop, mark your place.

4. Count the total number of words you read.

5. In the back of your Student Book, write the number of words you read and color in the squares on your Fluency Chart.

6. Now switch with your partner.

What Can Be Washed?

Hands:

Your hands can be washed. Washing your hands helps you stay well.

Clothes:

Your clothes can be washed. If mud gets on your pants or milk spills on your dresses, you can wash them. Washing your pants and dresses can help you not be a mess.

Pets:

Your pet can be washed. A washed dog will not have bugs and will smell fresh.

What can be washed? A lot!⑦⓪

The Ring

Stan had a gold ring. He put it in his sack and met his pals at the park. As they were swinging, the ring went clink and landed in the mud. It was missing! Stan yelled, "Help, the ring is lost!" The pals hunted for the ring. They dug in the mud and were in luck, but what a mess! They washed off the mud in the sink. His ring is now snug in a box by his bed.⑦⑨

A Pet Bath

If your pet rolls in the mud, he must have a bath. Fill up the tub. Then get him wet and wash and scrub him with warm suds. If he fusses, tell him no splashing, jumping, or kicking in the bath. He must sit still and be calm or suds will be spilled, and you will have a mess to mop. After your pet is washed, rub him with a cloth and then let him run.㊅

Chuck and Chip

Chuck the chimp sat on his branch thinking about what he would have for lunch. He wanted a big chunk of ham, nuts and chips that crunched, and some punch.

Then, his chum Chip jumped up. He was glum. "What is up?" said Chuck.

"I am sad," said Chip. "I have no lunch."

"Do not be sad," said Chuck. "I will be glad to share." And he did! The chimps munched their good lunch of ham, nuts, and chips.⑦⑨

Mom and Jen

"There is not one thing in the hutch to make for lunch," Mom said to Jen. "Look at the time on my watch! It is ten. We must fetch lunch and be back by one when Gram will come."

They jumped on a bus, but there was a hitch. The bus lost its clutch and ran into a ditch. They sat.

"What next?" said Mom.

A van honked. It was Gram! "Hop in," she said. "Let's go get lunch."⑦⑨

What to Make

What can you whip up when a chum stops by on a whim? It depends on the time. You can whisk some eggs in a pan. You can grill some ham. Put it on a wheat bun and add chips, and it will make a good lunch. What can you make after six? Whip up a little crab dip, and give him some fish. It will be good, and your chum will say yum!⑦⑷

Ann Is Queen

Ann sat in class for her quiz. She had to write a story and wanted to do her best. It was about a good king who went on a quest for a magic quilt and a quart of milk for a sick lad. When it was time to quit, all the kids wished their stories would be number one. The next day, her quiz was on her desk with the number one on it. Ann was best and was "Queen" for the day.⑧³

What Will You Write?

There are many things to write about. Some people like to tell a story. They may write about the wreck of a ship with lost gold or a king on a quest to halt men who do wrong. Other people like to write about things they know or do all the time. They may write about how to wrap a gift or how to tell time on a watch. We use writing all the time. What will you write?⑦⑨

Bob and the Knoll

Bob knelt to open the knot on his knapsack. He got a pen to write about all the things at the knoll for his report. A knoll is a small hill. Bob looked all over. He could see grass and rocks and many bugs and ants. He could see a fox in a log. He had his pad to write about it all. He went to class to tell his pals. It felt good to know more about the knoll.⑧⓪

The Zoo

There are many animals to see at the zoo.
These are a few:

- A big kangaroo who hops
- A troop of chimps on a branch
- Some chicks in a coop
- A wolf who snoops for food
- A smooth fox in a log
- A small owl who hoots on a stump
- A tiger who sits by a pool

What animal do you like best? Go to the
zoo and find out!⑦⑦

Pam's Sketch Book

Pam walked on the path by the brook to get to the zoo. Each day she stood and drew all the animals in her sketch book. The people who worked at the zoo asked to look and told her how good her work was. One day a chimp was missing. The zookeeper wanted her help. He took her sketches and put them up. Soon they got a call. They got the chimp back, and all was well thanks to Pam.⑧⓪

The Sad Ape

Abe the ape sat in his cage at the zoo. It was his home, and he liked it. He had a rope for swinging, branches to climb, and lots of food. He had a good life, but he was alone. He began to mope. The zookeeper knew that he was sad, and so he made some calls. One day Abe woke up. The gate swung wide and in came a new ape. At last, he had a mate. He was glad.(81)

The Pond

Bob went to look at the pond.

A frog hopped off a pad and landed in the water.

Bob looked past a log and saw a rat in the mud. Bob kicked a twig and the rat dashed off.㊴

Shop, Shop, Shop

People shop. Some people bring a list. Some do not.

Some people get bags and bags each trip. Some do not.

People shop.

"Mom shops for sales," said Peg.

"A good sale is fun to find," said Mom.

People shop.

"Dad shops for deals," said Tom.

"It is fun to find the best deal," said Dad.⑤⑥

Word List

there	people
many	been
see	some
come	now